PPC

Energy Essentials
Nuclear Energy

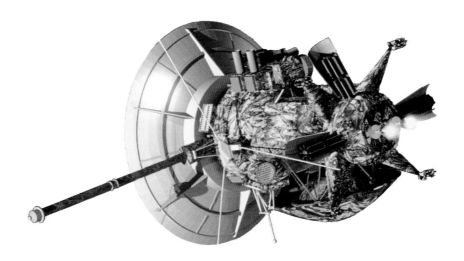

Nigel Saunders and Steven Chapman

www.raintreepublishers.co.uk
Visit our website to find out more information about **Raintree** books.

To order:
 Phone 44 (0) 1865 888113
Send a fax to 44 (0) 1865 314091
 Visit the Raintree Bookshop at **www.raintreepublishers.co.uk** to browse our catalogue and order online.

First published in Great Britain by Raintree,
Halley Court, Jordan Hill, Oxford OX2 8EJ, part of
Harcourt Education.
Raintree is a registered trademark of Harcourt Education Ltd.

Editorial: Charlotte Guillain and Isabel Thomas
Design: Michelle Lisseter and Bridge Creative Services Ltd
Picture Research: Maria Joannou and Catherine Bevan
Production: Jonathan Smith
Expert reader: Russell Suter
Index: Indexing Specialists (UK) Ltd
Nigel Saunders would like to thank Angela, Kathryn, David and Jean for their help and support.

Originated by Dot Gradations
Printed and bound in China by South China Printing Company

ISBN 1 844 43125 8
08 07 06 05 04
10 9 8 7 6 5 4 3 2 1

British Library Cataloguing in Publication Data
Saunders, Nigel and Chapman, Steven
Nuclear Energy
333.7'924
A full catalogue record for this book is available from the British Library.

Acknowledgements
pp.4/5, Photodisc; p.4, Tudor Photography; p.5, (top) Science Photo Library/Chris Butler; p.5, (middle) Science Photo Library; p.5, (bottom) Science Photo Library; p.6, (top) Photodisc; p.6, (bottom) Corbis; p.7, Science Photo Library/U.S. Dept. of Energy; pp.8–9, Science Photo Library; p.8, Science Photo Library; p.10, Photodisc; p.11, Science Photo Library; p.12, (top) Illustrated London News; p.12, (bottom) Science Photo Library/David Parker; p.13, (top) Science Photo Library; p.13, (bottom) Corbis; p.14, Science Photo Library; p.15, (top) National Air and Space Museum, Smithsonian Institute; p.15, (bottom) Science Photo Library; pp.16/17, Getty Images; p.16, Science Photo Library; p.17, Science Photo Library; pp.18/19, Science Photo Library; p.18, Science Photo Library; p.19, Rex Features/ Stock Medical; p.20, (top) Science Photo Library; p.21, Science Photo Library/Scott Camzine; pp.22/23, Corbis; p.22, Corbis; p.23, Photodisc; p.24 (right) Corbis/ Tim Wright; p.24, (left) Corbis; pp.26/27, Science Photo Library; p.26 Corbis; p.27, Australia Picture Library; p.28, (top) Science Photo Library; p.28, (bottom) Science Photo Library; p.29, Science Photo Library/Volker Steger; pp.30/31, U.S. Navy Visual News Service/ James Thierry; p.30, Corbis; p.31,Corbis; p.33, Science Photo Library; pp.34/35, Corbis; pp.34, Corbis; p.35, PA Photos/EPA; p.36, (top) Science Photo Library; p.36, (bottom) Science Photo Library; p.37, Corbis; p.38, Photodisc; p.39, NASA/HSTI; p.40, Science Photo Library; pp.40/41, PA Photos; p.41, Corbis; p.42, Corbis; p.43, (top) p.43, (bottom) Corbis; pp.44/45, Science Photo Library.

Cover photograph of Tokamak plasma reproduced with permission of Science Photo Library

Every effort has been made to contact copyright holders of any material reproduced in this book. Any omissions will be rectified in subsequent printings if notice is given to the publishers.

Contents

Any words appearing in the text in bold, **like this**, are explained in the Glossary. You can also look out for them in the Word store at the bottom of each page.

What is energy?

Energy for life

Food contains stored chemical energy. Our bodies break food down and release this energy in different forms. This energy keeps us warm. It lets our bodies move, mend injuries and grow. Without the energy from food, we could not live.

Energy is all around us. Without energy everything would be cold, dark, silent and still. Heat energy is what melts an ice cream on a sunny day and cooks our food. Light energy comes out of televisions, lamps and the Sun. Everything that moves, from a tiny bit of dust to a huge planet, has **kinetic energy**. Batteries store chemical energy and change it into electrical energy to power CD players and mobile phones.

Most of the energy needed for our everyday lives comes from **fuels**. Fuels are a store of energy. There are lots of different fuels, including wood, coal and petrol. These fuels store chemical energy, which is turned in to heat and light energy when they burn.

We get our energy from the food we eat.

Lightning contains huge amounts of energy.

Word store energy   ability to do work. Light, heat and electricity are types of energy.
fuel   substance that stores energy and releases it when it is burned

Nuclear energy

We can see or feel some types of energy. We can feel the warmth of the summer sun on our skin. Our eyes detect light energy and our ears detect sound energy. But there are some types of energy that we cannot see, hear or feel.

Microwave ovens cook food quickly, using invisible microwave energy. Radios tune in to invisible radio waves and the energy they carry. Nuclear energy is like this. It is invisible and silent and we cannot feel it. This book describes nuclear energy and what it can do for us.

Find out later ...

What do particle accelerators do?

How does nuclear energy affect living things?

What happens when a nuclear reactor explodes?

What is nuclear energy?

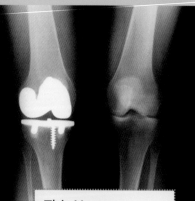

This X-ray photograph shows metal inside an artificial knee joint. ∧

To understand what nuclear energy is, it helps to know something about **radiation**. Light is one type of radiation, but there are many other types that are invisible to us. One of these was discovered by accident in 1896. A French scientist was doing experiments with a substance that glowed in the dark. This substance contained a metal called uranium. He wrapped a photographic plate (an early type of camera film) in paper and put a piece of the uranium-containing substance on top. When he developed the plate, he saw that the part next to the uranium had gone black.

Some invisible energy released by the uranium had gone straight through the paper and changed the photographic plate. It was a very exciting discovery. Scientists started to do experiments to find out more about this invisible energy.

X-rays

X-rays are another type of invisible radiation. They were discovered by Wilhelm Roentgen in 1895. He found that invisible energy rays came out of a machine he was using. This energy could pass through skin but not bone or metal. It also made photographic plates turn black. The very first X-ray photograph was of his wife's hand.

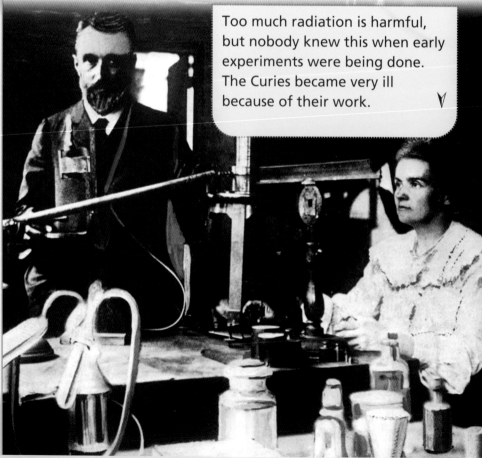

Too much radiation is harmful, but nobody knew this when early experiments were being done. The Curies became very ill because of their work. ∨

Word store

Latin   ancient language used by the Romans
radiation   type of energy in the form of rays, waves or particles

A curious glow in the dark

The scientists Marie and Pierre Curie did many experiments with substances containing uranium. In 1898, they discovered two new metals that gave off the invisible energy and also glowed in the dark. The Curies called this property **radioactivity**. Materials that give off this invisible radiation energy are said to be **radioactive**.

One of the new substances was named polonium, after Poland where Marie was born. The other was named radium, after the **Latin** word for **ray**.

Some radioactive substances give off so much energy that they glow in the dark. This is a lump of plutonium metal.

A deadly glow

In the early 1900s, radium paints were used to make watches glow in the dark. Water that contained radium was thought to be good for you, and you could buy soap and toothpaste with added radium. But many people fell ill and radium went out of fashion.

radioactive   something that can give off radiation
ray   beam of light or radiation

Each of these elements is made from a different type of atom. ∧

Inside the atom

To understand where invisible **radiation** comes from, it helps to know something about **atoms**.

Too small to see

Everything around us is made from tiny **particles** called atoms. These are far too small to see. Radium atoms are some of the largest atoms, but even a million of these would only be as wide as a human hair. There are over a hundred different types of atoms. About 90 of them are found naturally. Scientists have worked out how to make nearly 30 more.

For a long time, scientists thought that atoms were the smallest particles that existed. But in 1897, particles even smaller than atoms were discovered.

Elements and compounds

Elements are pure substances made from just one type of atom. Carbon is made from only carbon atoms. Oxygen is made from oxygen atoms. **Compounds** are made from two or more elements joined together. Water is a compound made from oxygen atoms and hydrogen atoms.

These are gold atoms on top of a sheet of carbon atoms. You cannot see atoms, but a special microscope, called a tunnelling electron microscope, can 'feel' them to make pictures like this. ➤

Word store atom   tiny particle that everything is made from
nuclear   anything to do with the nucleus of an atom

Inside the atom

Scientists now know that atoms are made from three types of incredibly tiny particles, called **sub-atomic particles**. The **electron** was the first sub-atomic particle to be discovered. The other two types were found later, at the start of the last century. They are called the **proton** and the **neutron**.

If you went inside an atom, you would come across clouds of electrons first. Much further inside is the **nucleus**. This is the middle of the atom. It is made from protons and neutrons joined together by very strong forces. When the nucleus of a large atom is split apart, or when two small **nuclei** are joined together, **nuclear** energy is given out.

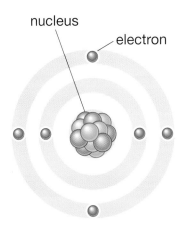

This is a model of a carbon atom. ∧

A model atom

The easiest way to imagine atoms and the sub-atomic particles is to think of them as tiny balls. There are different ideas, called models, about how electrons are arranged in an atom. In the simplest model, electrons move around the nucleus, a bit like the way the planets move around the Sun.

Crumbling atoms

The **protons** and **neutrons** in the **nucleus** of an **atom** are joined together by very strong forces. This means that the nucleus should not break up. But some atoms are naturally **unstable** and their **nuclei** can break up in to smaller pieces. When this happens, **nuclear** energy is given out in the form of **radiation**. These atoms are said to be **radioactive**.

Three types of radiation

Three main types of radiation are given out by radioactive atoms: alpha, beta and gamma. They are named after the first three letters of the Greek alphabet. The three types of radiation are very different from each other. Two are fast moving **sub-atomic particles** and the third is a type of invisible energy.

Graphite is a form of carbon used in pencils. Some types of carbon atoms have half-lives of less than a second. ∧

Half-life

Nobody can tell when a particular atom will break up. But scientists know that after a certain time, half of the atoms in a sample of radioactive material will have broken up. This time is called the **half-life** of the atom. Some types of atoms are very unstable and have half-lives of less than a second.

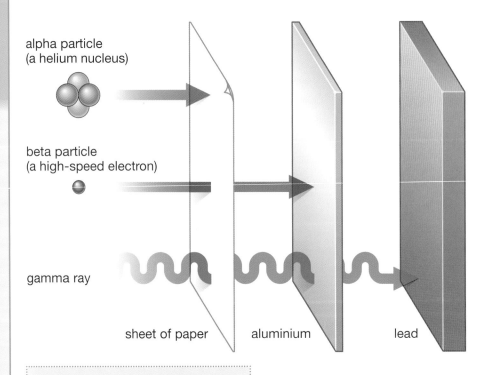

alpha particle
(a helium nucleus)

beta particle
(a high-speed electron)

gamma ray

sheet of paper   aluminium   lead

These are the three main types of radiation. They can all travel through air but are stopped by different substances. ∧

Word store   half-life   time it takes for half the atoms in a sample of radioactive material to break up

Alpha radiation

Alpha radiation is often written using the Greek letter α. It is made when a nucleus breaks up and fires out a tiny **particle**. This particle is made from two **protons** and two **neutrons** stuck together. This means an alpha particle is identical to the nucleus of a helium atom. It cannot travel very far in air and is easily stopped by a thin sheet of paper.

Beta radiation

Beta radiation can be written as β. It is made when a nucleus breaks up and fires out an **electron**. Although electrons are normally only found in clouds around the nucleus, they can also be made when a neutron turns into a proton. Beta radiation can travel through paper but is stopped by a thin sheet of aluminium metal.

Gamma radiation

Gamma radiation is often written as γ. Unlike alpha and beta radiation, it is not a type of sub-atomic particle. It is **rays** of invisible energy, like X-rays but much more powerful. Gamma radiation can pass through paper and aluminium, and is only stopped by thick sheets of lead or concrete.

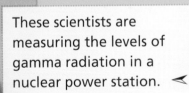

These scientists are measuring the levels of gamma radiation in a nuclear power station. ◄

Splitting atoms

Once scientists had found out about **atoms** that break up naturally, they wanted to know if atoms could be forced to break apart. They used **alpha radiation** to smash up atoms.

Tiny bullets

Light **radiation** moves so quickly that a **ray** of light from the Earth reaches the Moon in just 1.3 seconds. Alpha radiation also moves very fast. Scientists decided to use alpha radiation like tiny bullets. They wanted to fire the alpha **particles** at atoms to break them apart.

FAST FACTS
In a **vacuum**, light moves at 300,000,000 metres per second.

This is Albert Einstein (1879–1955). ⋏

Einstein and the speed of light

The scientist Albert Einstein came up with complex ideas about how the universe works. Einstein's Theory of Relativity says that nothing can move faster than the speed of light.

Scientists use huge machines, called **particle accelerators**, to get **sub-atomic particles** moving at high speeds before smashing them into each other. ➤

Word store   chemical reaction   reaction where the same elements join together in different ways

Splitting the atom

In 1919, the British scientist Ernest Rutherford managed to break atoms up. He aimed alpha radiation at nitrogen gas. When an alpha particle hit a nitrogen atom, the alpha particle and nitrogen **nucleus** stuck together for an instant. Then the whole thing flew apart, forming an oxygen atom and a **neutron** that shot away at high speed. This was called 'splitting the atom'.

Nuclear reactions

Splitting the atom is a type of **nuclear reaction**. It is called a nuclear reaction because an atom's nucleus has been changed. The atom changes from being one **element** to being a different element and nuclear energy is given out. By splitting many atoms at the same time, scientists were able to release enough energy to make an atomic bomb.

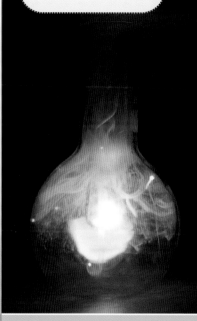

Sodium and chlorine react together to make sodium chloride, which we know as salt. ∨

Chemical reactions

A nuclear reaction is different from a **chemical reaction**. During a chemical reaction, an element cannot change into a different element. The same elements are there at the end of the reaction. They are just joined to each other in a different way.

nuclear reaction   reaction involving the nucleus of an atom
vacuum   empty space with nothing in it, not even air

The atomic bomb

When an **atom** breaks apart, **radiation** and heat energy are given out. Some **radioactive** substances, such as radium, are always warm because of this. To build an atomic bomb, scientists needed to make a lot of energy escape much more quickly. They had to find a way to split many atoms at once. Uranium was the substance they chose to do this.

Why uranium?

Atoms of a type of uranium called uranium-235 are especially easy to split. If a **neutron** moving at high speed hits a uranium-235 **nucleus**, the nucleus breaks up into two smaller **nuclei**. When this happens, **gamma radiation** and heat energy are produced. At the same time, two or three more neutrons shoot out at high speed. Splitting atoms is also called **nuclear fission**.

This is the Trinity bomb before it exploded. ⋀

The first atomic bomb

The Manhattan Project was set up during World War Two. It built the world's first atomic bomb, code-named Trinity. This was tested in New Mexico in the USA on 16 July 1945. The explosion was as powerful as 20,000 tonnes of high explosive.

This diagram shows how nuclear fission works. ⋁

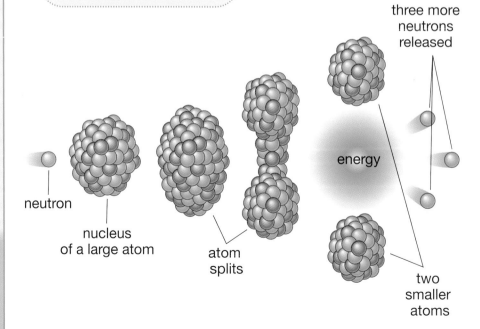

three more neutrons released

energy

neutron

nucleus of a large atom

atom splits

two smaller atoms

Chain reactions

Each of the new neutrons strikes another uranium-235 nucleus. And each of these breaks apart too, releasing more neutrons. The **nuclear reactions** get faster and faster as more uranium atoms split, releasing even more neutrons. This is called a **chain reaction**.

If there is not enough uranium, the neutrons just escape and the chain reaction stops. If there is just enough uranium, called the **critical mass**, the reaction keeps happening quite slowly. But if there is more than the critical mass of uranium, something else happens.

Atomic bombs

Above the critical mass, the nuclear reaction gets faster and faster. It gives out so much energy in a short time that a nuclear explosion happens.

The atomic bomb used in Hiroshima showed the world how powerful nuclear energy could be. ʌ

War with atomic bombs

The first atomic bomb used in a war was dropped by the USA during the Second World War. The bomb exploded over Hiroshima in Japan on 6 August 1945. Buildings were flattened and over 130,000 people were killed or injured in just a few seconds.

The world's first atomic bomb was tested in 1945 making this huge fireball. ◄

critical mass   amount of radioactive metal needed for a steady nuclear reaction
nuclear fission   splitting atoms

15

Radiation and living things

There are many **radioactive** substances in the world. The **radiation** they give out is all around us and is called **background radiation**.

Radioactive rocks

When the Earth was formed about 4.5 **billion** years ago, it contained a lot of radioactive **elements**. Most of these quickly broke down into elements that were not radioactive. But others, such as uranium, are still found in the ground today.

Radioactive rocks such as granite contain uranium. The uranium in them breaks down to make other radioactive substances. One of these is a gas called radon. It can get into houses through cracks in floors and walls. In areas at risk from radon, people are given help to protect their homes.

This device is used to detect dangerous radiation levels. ∧

Radon at home

Radon is heavier than air, so it stays in the basement of a house and can build up to dangerous levels. A 'radon sump' can be fitted to trap the radon. Ventilation fans then send the radon outside, where it escapes into the air.

The amount of background radiation you are exposed to depends on where you live, your job and what you eat. The pie chart shows the average contributions that different sources make to background radiation in the UK. ➤

Word store background radiation   radiation that is all around us
billion   one thousand million

Swallowing radiation

As plants grow, they take in **minerals** from the soil. Some of these are radioactive, so the plants become slightly radioactive too. When animals eat these plants, they also become slightly radioactive. When we eat food or have a drink, these radioactive substances go into us, too. But do not panic – the amounts are very small.

Radiation from the sky

Another source of natural radiation is cosmic rays from space. They are made up of **gamma radiation** and fast-moving **sub-atomic particles** such as **protons** and alpha particles. The Earth's magnetic field and atmosphere stop a lot of these rays from reaching the surface of our planet.

We cannot escape from background radiation and our bodies can cope with it. But a big dose of radiation can be harmful and even **fatal**.

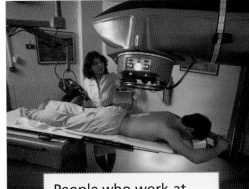

People who work at nuclear power stations, people who take X-rays at hospitals and some scientists are at risk from radiation. ⋀

Checking radiation

Some jobs put people at risk of being exposed to a big dose of radiation. These people often wear a badge containing a piece of film that monitors their dose of radiation over time. The film will turn black if there is dangerous radiation around.

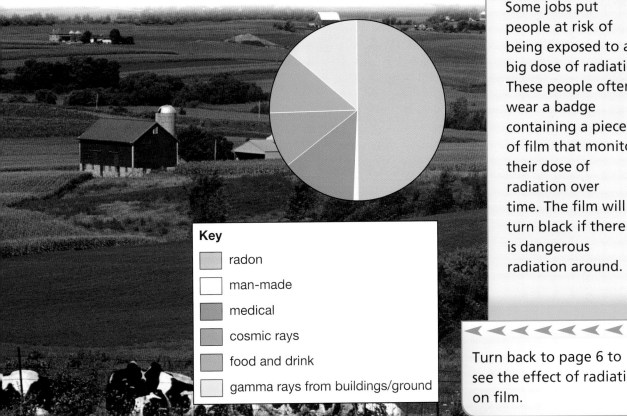

Key
- radon
- man-made
- medical
- cosmic rays
- food and drink
- gamma rays from buildings/ground

◀ ◀ ◀ ◀ ◀ ◀ ◀ ◀

Turn back to page 6 to see the effect of radiation on film.

fatal   something that kills you
mineral   substance needed by plants and animals in small amounts to keep them healthy

Mutation

Some changes to DNA cause **mutations**. These can alter the way an animal or plant looks, or the way it behaves. Mutations happen naturally and many are harmless. But some are very harmful. Being exposed to radiation increases the chance of mutation happening in a cell.

Nuclear energy and living things

In the same way that a wall is made from lots of bricks, living things are made from lots of tiny units called **cells**. **Radiation** can damage or kill cells, making us ill.

Crashing into cells

Radiation can damage things that it comes into contact with. Invisible ultraviolet radiation from the Sun damages plastic. It makes the plastic slowly crumble and change colour. It can burn our skin if we do not wear sunscreen. Radiation can also damage substances inside our cells, including our **DNA**.

DNA is a complex chemical that carries **genetic** information. Every cell uses this information as instructions to make the substances it needs to do its job properly. If the DNA is damaged by radiation, the information gets muddled. The cell stops working properly and may die.

FAST FACTS
DNA stands for deoxyribonucleic acid.

This mutant fruit fly has four wings instead of two. ⋀

cancer   disease caused by cells growing out of control
cell   tiny object that living things are made from

Not all radiation is the same

Alpha, **beta** and **gamma radiation** have different effects on cells. Their effects also depend on whether the **radioactive** source is outside or inside the body.

Alpha radiation is the least dangerous type of radioactive radiation when it is outside the body. It is usually stopped by the top layers of skin, where the cells are already dead. But it is different if the radioactive source is swallowed or breathed in. Then, alpha radiation is the most dangerous type because the particles are large and harm DNA easily.

Beta and gamma radiation are more dangerous than alpha radiation when they are outside the body. They are less dangerous than alpha radiation when they are inside the body because they pass out of the body quickly.

When you go out in the sun, slip on a shirt, slop on some sun block and slap on a hat. ∧

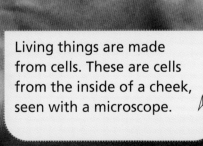

Living things are made from cells. These are cells from the inside of a cheek, seen with a microscope. ∧

Sunbathing

Sunshine is not just light radiation. It also contains some types of invisible radiation. We feel **infra-red** radiation on our skin as heat. We cannot feel ultraviolet radiation, but it can damage skin cells. Skin turns darker to try to block the ultraviolet rays. But a tan is a sign of damaged skin and too much sunbathing can cause skin **cancer**.

DNA   chemical that carries information that cells need to work properly
genetic   to do with information in cells

Nuclear medicine

Sometimes the damage that **radiation** does to **DNA** makes **cells** grow out of control, causing **cancer**. But like all cells, cancer cells in **tumours** can be killed by high doses of radiation.

Treating cancer with radiation

A **radioactive** material is sealed in a needle. The doctor puts this in the tumour or near it. The radiation kills cancer cells without harming too many normal cells around the tumour. Sometimes powerful X-rays or gamma **rays** are aimed at the tumour. Small **particle accelerators** may also be used. They fire high-speed **neutrons** or other **sub-atomic particles** at the tumour.

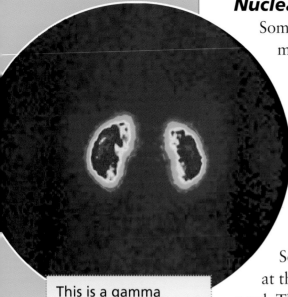

This is a gamma scan of two healthy kidneys, seen from behind. ⋀

Scanning for disease

To make a **gamma scan**, a small amount of a radioactive tracer is injected into the patient. The tracer builds up in the part of the body that the doctor wants to study. A machine detects gamma rays from the tracer and makes a picture.

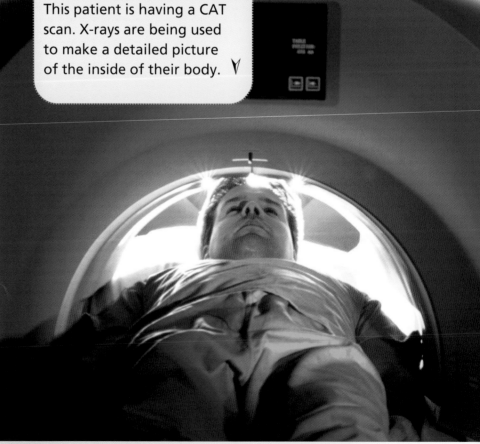

This patient is having a CAT scan. X-rays are being used to make a detailed picture of the inside of their body. ⋁

Word store   irradiated   exposed to radiation
sterilized   object without any living bacteria on or in it

Seeing inside

Doctors also use radiation to find out what is wrong with their patients. **Radioactive** substances called **tracers** are used to scan for diseases. Different tracers travel to different parts of the body, such as the bones, heart, brain or liver. They give off low-energy gamma rays that are easily detected by a scanner but do not harm the patient. The substances used have a short **half-life**, which is long enough to examine the patient without giving them a high dose of radiation.

CAT scans

CAT scans are very detailed X-ray photographs that look like slices through the body. A lot of weak X-rays are sent through a part of the patient and detected by the scanner. A computer turns the information from the X-rays into a picture.

Irradiated food must have this radura logo, or be labelled 'irradiated' or 'treated with ionising radiation'. ⋀

Sterile

Very high doses of ultraviolet, X-ray or **gamma radiation** can kill harmful bacteria. **Surgical instruments** and other hospital equipment can be **sterilized** using radiation. In some countries, food is **irradiated** to kill bacteria so it can be stored for longer without going bad.

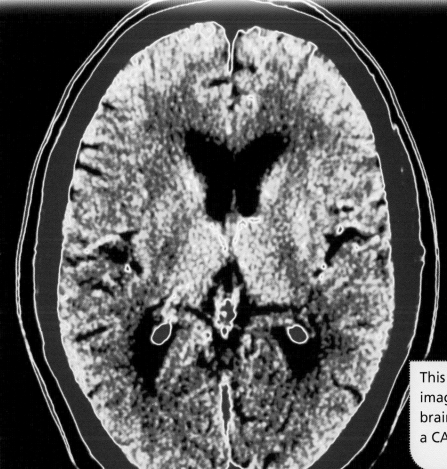

This photo shows an image inside the brain, taken using a CAT scan. ⋖

tracer   substance that is easy to track inside the body
tumour   lump caused by cancer cells

Nuclear power

Heat is given out by the **radioactive** substances in rocks deep inside the Earth. Without this heat, the inside of the Earth would have cooled very quickly after it formed. This heat keeps part of the **Earth's core** liquid, which is important for making the Earth's magnetic field.

Volcano!

Heat energy from radioactive substances melts rocks underground. In some parts of the world, this hot liquid rock pushes up through the Earth's crust, bringing the heat energy to the surface in volcanoes. Volcanoes eventually cool down. But before this happens, we can use the heat energy from the rocks around them.

The Roman baths at Bath in the UK. ⋏

Hot Bath

Hot rocks can warm up water running through them. Where this happens, a hot **spring** can form. In Bath in the UK, the ancient Romans built a pool filled by a hot spring. A million litres of water at 46 °C still comes out of the spring every day.

This is a geothermal power station in Iceland. The waste water from the power station is warm, and people can play in it. ⋏

expand   get bigger
generator   equipment used to make electricity

Electricity from steam

In power stations, **fossil fuels** are burned to boil water and make steam. The steam turns a **turbine**. This is a bit like a complex windmill with many blades. Instead of being turned by the wind, it is turned by fast moving steam. The turbine is connected to an electricity **generator**. The turbine turns the generator, which makes electricity.

Geothermal energy

In some places, hot rocks underground heat nearby water to make steam. By drilling a well, it is possible to bring this steam up to the surface. **Geothermal** power stations use the steam to turn electricity generators. They do not need any fuel and they do not make any harmful **waste**. But hot rocks are not found everywhere in the world. Iceland uses a lot of geothermal energy, but the world's biggest geothermal power station is at The Geysers in California. It makes enough electricity for a big city.

Geysers

Sometimes hot rocks heat water in a deep well to a temperature above its normal boiling point. The water **expands** and rises to the surface, where it boils. Hot water and steam are sprayed high into the air. This is called a geyser.

The Old Faithful geyser in the USA can reach 56 metres high.

geothermal   anything to do with heat from deep underground
turbine   machinery that is turned by moving air, water or steam

23

Layer 7 SP1 Graphite
Layer 6 4½" Cylinders Black Oxide

Nuclear reactors

Geothermal power stations can only be used in places with suitable hot rocks. In the 1950s, scientists decided to find a way to make machines that would do the same job as the hot rocks. These would have to produce **nuclear reactions** to heat water and make steam. The **nuclear reactor** was invented.

First choose your radioactive substance

Most **radioactive** substances are not right for powering a nuclear reactor. They give off heat too slowly or too quickly, or they cannot keep a **chain reaction** going. The builders of the first atomic bomb chose uranium-235. This is also used in most nuclear reactors. Its **atoms** can be split easily using **neutrons**.

The uranium in a nuclear reactor is called the **fuel**, even though it is not burned. The nuclear reaction in the fuel must be controlled. If it goes too slowly, not enough heat will be produced. If it goes too quickly, a massive nuclear explosion could happen.

The top of a nuclear reactor. ⩒

control rod   part of a nuclear reactor that controls the speed of the reaction
nuclear reactor   structure for making heat using radioactive substances

Control that reaction

The speed of the reaction is controlled using **control rods**. They usually contain boron or cadmium. These elements mop up free neutrons, stopping them from splitting more uranium atoms. If the control rods are lifted out of the fuel, less neutrons are mopped up and the reaction goes faster. It goes slower if the control rods are lowered. Neutrons have to be going at the correct speed to split uranium atoms. Blocks of **graphite** in the reactor slow neutrons to the right speed.

Grab that heat

The fuel, control rods and graphite make up the **reactor core**. This is put in a strong steel container called the **reactor vessel**. A thick concrete shield stops **radiation** escaping to the outside. A gas or liquid called the **coolant** takes heat from the reactor core to the outside, where it can be used to heat water and drive a **generator**.

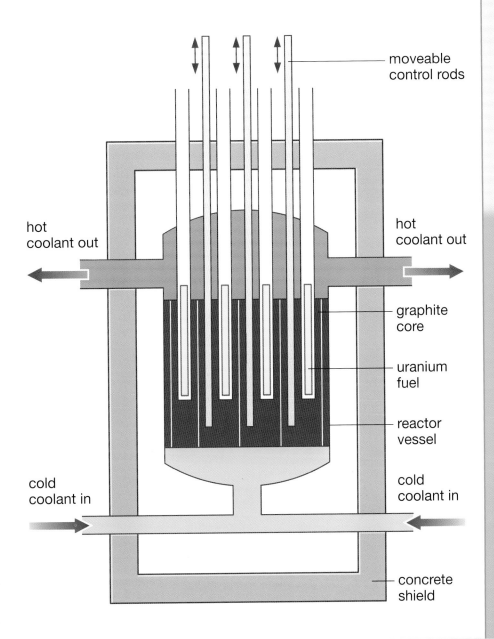

moveable control rods

hot coolant out

hot coolant out

graphite core

uranium fuel

reactor vessel

cold coolant in

cold coolant in

concrete shield

There are many different designs of nuclear reactor. This diagram shows the main parts of one.

reactor core   main part of a nuclear reactor
reactor vessel   container for the reactor core

The Calder Hall nuclear power station in 1957. ⋀

Making electricity

Power stations can be fuelled with coal, oil, natural gas or uranium. It does not matter which **fuel** a power station uses – in each case the fuel gives out heat energy that is used to boil water and make steam. This turns a **turbine**, which turns an electricity **generator**.

Heat is taken from the core of a **nuclear reactor** using a **coolant** gas or liquid. The coolant becomes **radioactive** as it goes around inside the **reactor core**. It is important that the coolant does not escape or mix with the water used to make steam. So one set of pipes carries the coolant and another set of pipes carries the water. The two sets of pipes are placed close to each other so that the heat passes from the coolant to the water.

The first nuclear power station

The first nuclear power station in the world was the Magnox reactor at Calder Hall in north-west England. It was opened by Queen Elizabeth II in 1956 and made enough electricity for a large city. It was closed down in 2003 because it was too expensive to operate. It will take 100 years to make the site safe again.

FAST FACTS
The transfer of heat between the coolant and water is called heat exchange.

AGR   advanced gas-cooled reactor
efficient   able to do a job without wasting a lot of energy

Different coolants

Water is the coolant in most of the world's nuclear power stations. Over half use Pressurised Water Reactors, or **PWRs**. The coolant water in a PWR is under high pressure. This lets it reach 325 °C without boiling.

The coolant in some reactors is carbon dioxide gas. The first gas-cooled reactor was called Magnox. A more **efficient** design, called the Advanced Gas-cooled Reactor, or **AGR**, is only used in the UK.

Mining uranium

Nuclear reactors need up to 100 tonnes of fuel every couple of years, so where does it come from? Australia has no nuclear power stations but its mines supply 28 per cent of the world's uranium. Kazakhstan, Canada, South Africa and Namibia supply most of the rest.

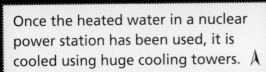

This is a uranium mine in Australia. ∧

Once the heated water in a nuclear power station has been used, it is cooled using huge cooling towers. ∧

Nuclear power in space

Spacecraft need a supply of energy for all the equipment they carry. The space shuttle uses **fuel cells** to make the electricity it needs. These are powered by hydrogen and oxygen. Satellites in orbit around the Earth have large panels of solar cells. These change energy from sunlight into electricity. But spacecraft may go so far from the Sun that their solar cells cannot make enough electricity. They cannot carry enough fuel to keep fuel cells running either. These spacecraft use nuclear energy instead.

Getting warm

Radioactive substances release some heat energy. If a substance containing **curium** is dissolved in water, so much heat is given off that the mixture starts to boil. Spacecraft can use this heat energy.

This is a Russian Lunokhod moon rover. ʌ

Keeping warm on the Moon

When Russia sent robot **rovers** to the Moon in the 1970s, it needed to stop delicate equipment freezing in the cold **lunar** night. The **alpha radiation** released by polonium can heat the metal to above 500 °C. The moon rovers were kept warm using polonium.

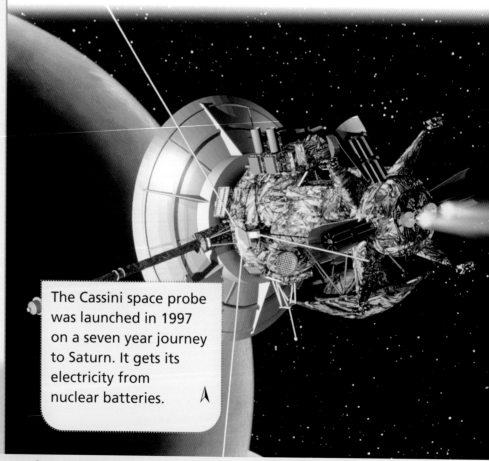

The Cassini space probe was launched in 1997 on a seven year journey to Saturn. It gets its electricity from nuclear batteries. ʌ

curium   very radioactive rare metal
fuel cell   device that makes electricity using chemical reactions

Electricity from heat

An **RTG** is a type of nuclear battery. It changes heat energy from a radioactive substance into electrical energy. RTGs are small and do not add much to a spacecraft's weight. They have no moving parts, so they are unlikely to go wrong. This is important when the nearest mechanics are millions of kilometres away!

Most RTGs are powered by plutonium-238. This has a **half-life** of 88 years, so it will give off energy for a long time. This is important for missions that last many years. Plutonium-238 is safer than curium, which gives off more harmful **gamma radiation** as well as heat. This might harm the spacecraft's builders.

What happens if it crashes?

In 1978, a Russian satellite called Cosmos 954 fell out of orbit and crashed in Canada. It was powered by uranium and the crash spread **radioactive** substances over more than 100,000 square kilometres (38,000 square miles). It cost six million dollars to clean up the wreck.

A satellite re-entering the Earth's atmosphere. ⋁

rover   moving machine for collecting information about a planet or moon
RTG   short for radioisotope thermoelectric generator, a type of nuclear battery

Nuclear power at sea

Submarines spend most of their time underwater, where they are difficult for an enemy to find. If they have to come to the surface to refuel they are easily found. Nuclear-powered submarines can stay underwater for many months. They only need to surface to stock up on food for the crew.

Just 1 kilogram of uranium is enough to make as much electricity as 10 tonnes of oil. This means that a ship or submarine powered by a **nuclear reactor** needs to carry very little **fuel**. Special small nuclear reactors are used instead of the large versions found in power stations.

Two nuclear-powered submarines at the North Pole.

Pushing through ice

The USS *Nautilus* was the world's first nuclear-powered submarine. In 1959, the USS *Skate* went on a trip of more than 5000 kilometres (3000 miles). It was the first submarine to surface through the ice at the North Pole.

cargo ship   ship that carries goods around the world
icebreaker   ship that clears ice from the surface of the sea

On the sea

The USS *Enterprise* was the world's first nuclear-powered aircraft carrier. It was launched in 1961 and it has eight nuclear reactors. Modern designs usually have just two reactors. These only need refuelling every ten years. So why are there only about 150 nuclear-powered ships in the world?

Nuclear-powered ships cost a lot of money to build and run. Many ports will only allow nuclear-powered ships to dock after lots of safety checks have been carried out. Only three nuclear-powered **cargo ships** have ever been built. Two of them worked well but cost too much to run, while the third kept going wrong.

This is a nuclear-powered icebreaker on its way to the North Pole. ∧

Icebreakers

In very cold parts of the world, **shipping lanes** get blocked by sheets of ice on the ocean surface. **Icebreakers** are very powerful and tough ships that can break through ice. Russia has several nuclear-powered icebreakers.

The USS *Enterprise*, the world's first nuclear-powered aircraft carrier. ◄

shipping lane   route taken by ships from one port to another

An energy alternative?

Going up

Going up

During the last 200 years, the concentration of carbon dioxide in the atmosphere has gone up. The Earth's average temperature has also risen, making the water in the seas and oceans expand. Some of the ice covering the land in cold places has melted and the average sea level has gone up.

Nuclear power stations make 17 per cent of the world's electricity. Nearly all the rest comes from power stations that burn **fossil fuels** (coal, oil and natural gas) to heat water. Each type of **fuel** has its own benefits and problems. All of them damage the environment.

The greenhouse effect

The Sun's heat energy keeps the surface of the Earth warm. Without the Earth's atmosphere, most of the Sun's heat energy would escape back into space. Certain gases in the atmosphere stop heat escaping back into space. These **greenhouse gases** keep the Earth warm enough for living things. This is called the **greenhouse effect**.

As the amount of carbon dioxide in the atmosphere has gone up, so has the average temperature. ➢

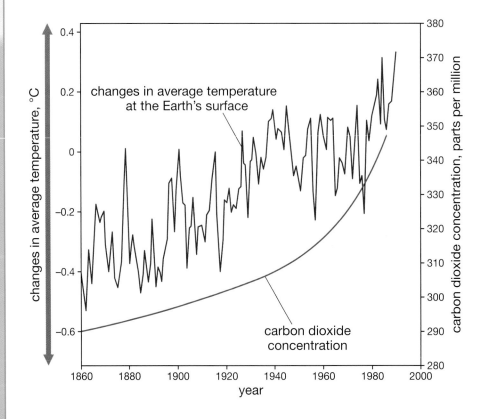

global warming   extra warming of the Earth caused by an increased greenhouse effect

Global warming

The fossil fuels give out carbon dioxide when they burn. Carbon dioxide is a greenhouse gas. During the last 200 years, the concentration of carbon dioxide in the atmosphere has gone up. This has made the greenhouse effect bigger than it should be. The Earth's average temperature has risen. This is called **global warming**.

A nuclear future?

Nuclear power stations do not release any greenhouse gases. Some scientists and politicians believe that the world should make more of its electricity using **nuclear reactors**, instead of burning fossil fuels. They hope that this will reduce global warming. But other people are worried about nuclear power.

In the greenhouse

Global warming is starting to change the world's weather. Some parts of the world are getting more rain than they did 50 years ago, while other parts are starting to get less rain. The **polar ice caps** are melting. Over the last 100 years, the sea level has gone up by at least 10 centimetres. If this continues, many lowland areas will be flooded.

Fossil fuels give off smoke and harmful gases when they burn. Nuclear power stations do not.

This bar chart shows how much electricity is made by nuclear power stations in the USA, UK and France. Australia has no nuclear power stations.

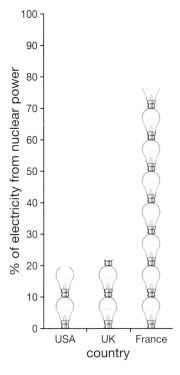

greenhouse effect   keeping the atmosphere warm by trapping heat
greenhouse gas   gas that is good at trapping heat

A blue glow

Used nuclear fuel is very radioactive because nuclear reactions make lots of new radioactive substances. It also keeps giving off heat and light energy. Most used fuel is stored in water for several years. During this time, it cools down and becomes less radioactive.

Problems, problems ...

Building more **nuclear** power stations, and closing down power stations that use **fossil fuels**, might help to stop **global warming**. So why are many people worried about this idea? The answer lies in the dangers of **radioactive** fuels and **wastes**.

Radioactive reactors

Nuclear fuels give off **radiation** during **nuclear reactions**. But this does not mean that they stop being radioactive. Radiation from the fuel also makes other substances in the reactor very radioactive. This includes the **coolant**, all the tubes, the rest of the core and the **reactor vessel** itself. When a nuclear power station is closed down, or **decommissioned**, the reactor is carefully taken apart and most of the radioactive material is buried deep underground.

Radiation from used fuel makes water in the cooling pond glow blue. ∧

decommissioned   taken out of service and closed down
reprocessing   making new nuclear fuel from used nuclear fuel

Used fuel

Used fuel is still very radioactive. It can be made into a dry powder and sealed in glass. This radioactive glass is stored in metal containers. But used fuel still contains small amounts of useful uranium and plutonium. These can be taken out and made into new fuel. Reprocessing makes even more liquid and solid radioactive waste.

Hide it away

Radioactive substances in nuclear waste can have very long **half-lives**. They will stay radioactive for thousands of years. Waste that is not very radioactive is usually buried in the ground in metal containers. Highly radioactive waste is more difficult to deal with. Scientists are looking for new places where it can be buried without harming living things or the environment.

These people in France are protesting about nuclear waste. ∧

Not in my back yard!

Many people are worried about radiation. They would not be happy to live near a nuclear power station or for radioactive waste to be buried nearby. People all around the world have **protested** to keep these things away from their homes.

Radioactive substances are labelled with a warning sign. Metal containers of radioactive waste are usually buried underground. ∢

waste   unwanted material left behind

When things go wrong

If things go wrong with a **nuclear reactor**, there is always the danger that **radioactive** substances will escape.

Fire!

In 1957, there was a fire at a UK reactor that made plutonium for atomic bombs from uranium. The **graphite** core caught fire. This melted the uranium **fuel** and also set light to it. Radioactive smoke escaped into the air before the fire could be put out. Milk from farms within 500 square kilometres (190 square miles) was banned because radioactive substances fell on the grass. But the fire led scientists and engineers to design safer reactors.

An accident at the Chernobyl nuclear power station destroyed the reactor and let out huge amounts of radioactive substances. ➢

Three Mile Island

In 1979, a nuclear power station in Pennsylvania in the USA went wrong. A small fault made the reactor start to shut down. It was designed to do this, but something went wrong with the cooling system. Most of the coolant water boiled away and some of the fuel melted.

meltdown   when nuclear fuel gets so hot that it melts

The Chernobyl disaster

The **nuclear reaction** in a nuclear reactor is controlled using **control rods**. When some rods are lifted out, the reaction speeds up. But what happens if nearly all of them are lifted out at once?

In 1986, an experiment in a nuclear power station went badly wrong. The reactor was near Chernobyl in the Ukraine. It had 211 control rods and needed 30 in the reactor to be safe. Mistakes were made that left just eight control rods in the reactor. The nuclear reaction went out of control. So much heat was given off that there was a **meltdown** and the **coolant** water boiled. Pressure from the steam caused an explosion that blew off the reactor lid. The graphite core caught fire and enormous amounts of radioactive substances escaped.

After Chernobyl

It took several days to put out the fires in the Chernobyl reactor. The wind carried radioactive substances all over Europe and even to some parts of the USA. Three million people in the Ukraine were exposed to the **radioactivity**, and over 4000 of the clean-up workers have died from the effects.

Pripyat, a town near the wrecked Chernobyl reactor, is still abandoned.

Turn back to page 25 to recall how control rods control nuclear reactions.

Nuclear fusion

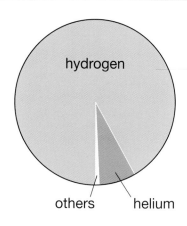

hydrogen

others   helium

This pie chart shows what type of atoms are in the Sun.

What is the Sun?

The Sun is over a million times bigger than the Earth. Nearly all the atoms in the Sun are hydrogen or helium, and there are all sorts of sub-atomic particles whizzing around in it. Its centre is 30,000 times hotter than an oven.

FAST FACTS

Fission means splitting and fusion means joining together.

The Sun is the nearest star to the Earth. It produces the light and heat energy needed by living things. Without the Sun's light, plants could not make food and we would starve. The Sun's heat drives our weather and the water cycle that causes rain. All this energy comes from **nuclear reactions** in the Sun.

Fission and fusion

Nuclear power stations use a type of reaction called **nuclear fission**. This is when the **nucleus** of a large **atom** breaks apart, making two smaller atoms and releasing lots of nuclear energy, which is used to heat water. A different type of reaction, called **nuclear fusion**, happens in the Sun.

In nuclear fusion, two small atoms hit each other with so much force that their **nuclei** join together. This makes a bigger nucleus and gives off **radiation** energy.

When seen from a satellite in space, our Sun is a huge ball of swirling hot gases.

gravity   force that pulls everything together and keeps us on the ground
nuclear fusion   nuclear reaction where the nuclei of two atoms join together

Nuclear fusion in the Sun

In the centre of the Sun the temperatures and pressures are huge. They make hydrogen **atoms** join together to form helium atoms. This reaction gives off large amounts of radiation, including fast-moving **sub-atomic particles**. It also gives off **infra-red** radiation, which we feel as heat, and light radiation. The Sun is like a gigantic nuclear explosion happening in front of us.

A balancing act

The Sun is huge. Its **gravity** is so strong that even escaping gases are pulled back in. When we look at photographs of the Sun, we see the result of a balancing act between the energy released by **nuclear fusion** and gravity.

When stars die

Our Sun is about halfway through its life. It will run out of hydrogen **fuel** in five **billion** years time. Different fusion reactions will start in it. The Sun will get hotter and bigger, and it may destroy the Earth.

A supernova happens when an old star explodes. ◄

Making a Sun on the Earth

The Sun fuses hydrogen **atoms** to give off huge amounts of nuclear energy. The Earth has a lot of water in its oceans, and water contains hydrogen atoms. If scientists and engineers can make **nuclear fusion** reactors, the world could have enough **fuel** to release energy almost forever. Nuclear fusion has already happened on the Earth. But it made explosions, not electricity.

The hydrogen bomb

The world's first hydrogen bomb was tested in 1952 by the USA. It exploded at Eniwetok Atoll in the Pacific Ocean. The explosion was hundreds of times more powerful than the atomic bomb that destroyed Hiroshima in 1945. It destroyed an island and left a crater 50 metres deep. Since then, even more powerful hydrogen bombs have been tested by the USA and other countries.

Banning the Bomb

Because of worries about radioactive **fallout** and nuclear war, many countries agreed to a Comprehensive Test **Ban** Treaty in 1996. This bans nuclear **weapon tests** anywhere on the planet.

This huge crater in the Nevada Desert in the USA was made when a nuclear bomb was tested in 1962. ∨

Word store   ban   not allow something to happen
fallout   substances that are made in an explosion and fall to the ground

Fusion power

Scientists and engineers have been very successful at using nuclear fusion to make bombs. But they are are finding it more difficult to use it to make electricity. There are many problems, and researching how to solve them is expensive.

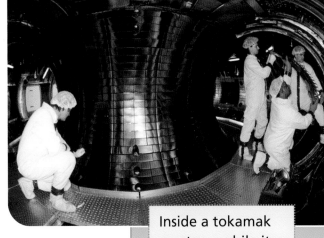

Inside a tokamak reactor – while it is not running! ⋀

Very high temperatures get fusion reactions going in the Sun. It is difficult to heat hydrogen fuel to these temperatures on the Earth without destroying the reactor. It will take many years before we can build a fusion reactor that is big enough to give out more energy than it uses at start-up. Then there is another problem: once a fusion reactor starts up it becomes very **radioactive**, just like the reactors in ordinary nuclear power stations.

Doughnut power

The most popular fusion reactor design is called a tokamak, which is shaped like a hollow doughnut. The fuel is heated by microwave radiation, and powerful magnetic fields keep the hot fuel away from the walls of the reactor.

Many people want to see nuclear weapons banned and taken apart. ≺

Nuclear power in the future

Laser fusion

Lasers make beams of concentrated light or heat energy. Scientists have used very powerful lasers to squeeze liquid hydrogen so much that **nuclear fusion** begins. The equipment is very large at the moment, but future research might lead to nuclear fusion power stations.

As with all the different ways to make electricity, nuclear power has its benefits and its problems.

Benefits

- Nuclear power stations produce a large amount of energy from a very small amount of **fuel**.
- They do not produce any **greenhouse gases**, unlike power stations fuelled by coal, oil or natural gas. Making electricity using nuclear power stations, instead of using coal-fired power stations, prevents over 2 **billion** tonnes of carbon dioxide going into the atmosphere every year. This helps to slow down **global warming**.
- Nuclear power stations are very reliable and easy to run and maintain.

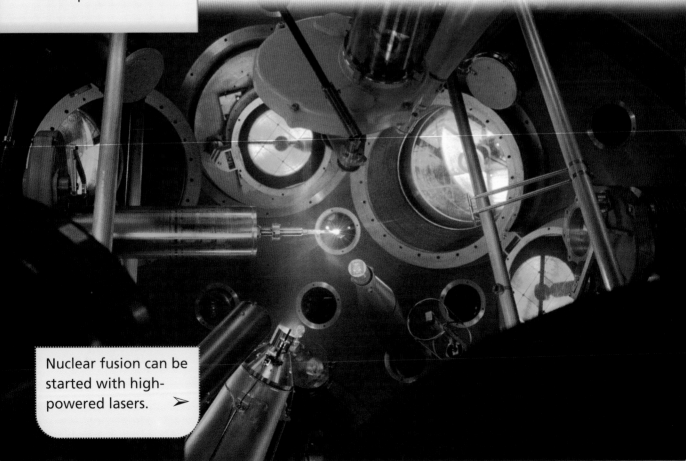

Nuclear fusion can be started with high-powered lasers. ➤

Word store   contaminated spoiled
predict   make an informed guess that something will happen

Problems

- Nuclear power stations do not go wrong very often. But if a big accident happens, like the Chernobyl disaster, the results are very serious. Large areas can be **contaminated** with **radioactive** substances.
- Nuclear power stations make **waste** that stays radioactive for a long time. For example, the plutonium in used nuclear fuel will still be dangerous to living things in 250,000 years.
- Nuclear waste is very hard to store safely. Scientists are having difficulties finding suitable places to bury it. A burial site must be safe from earthquakes or water running through it for many thousands of years. But nobody can really **predict** what will happen to the waste in the future.
- It is difficult and expensive to make an old reactor safe.
- There is only enough uranium on Earth to last about 65 years. Once we have used it all, it will be gone for ever.

Nuclear missile nose cones being blown up. ⋀

Going ... and not going

Some countries are trying to make nuclear weapons, while other countries are trying to stop this happening. Some, including the USA and Russia, have broken up a number of their own nuclear weapons. Overall there are fewer nuclear weapons than there used to be.

The French Superphoenix nuclear reactor was an advanced design. It used liquid sodium metal as its **coolant**, but it was closed down because of leaks. ⋖

Find out more

Organizations

British Nuclear Fuels

Go to the Education section for information about the good side of nuclear energy.
bnfl.com

Greenpeace

This site has lots of information about the problems with nuclear energy.
greenpeace.org/nuclear/

Uranium

Information about the background radiation around us from the Australian Uranium Information Centre.
uic.com.au/ral.htm

Books

Science Topics: Energy, Chris Oxlade
(Heinemann Library, 2000)
Energy for Life: Nuclear Energy, Robert Sneddon
(Heinemann Library, 2002)

World Wide Web

If you want to find out more about **nuclear energy**, you can search the Internet using keywords like these:

- nuclear + [name of country]
- 'nuclear fission'
- 'nuclear fusion'
- 'nuclear power'
- 'nuclear reactor'
- radiation
- radioactivity
- uranium + fuel
- Chernobyl + nuclear

You can also find your own keywords by using headings or words from this book. Use the search tips opposite to help you find the most useful websites.

Search tips

There are billions of pages on the Internet so it can be difficult to find exactly what you are looking for. For example, if you just type in 'energy' on a search engine like Google, you will get a list of 35 million web pages. These search skills will help you find useful websites more quickly:

- Use simple keywords instead of whole sentences
- Use two to six keywords in a search, putting the most important words first
- Be precise – only use names of people, places or things
- If you want to find words that go together, put quote marks around them, for example 'nuclear energy' or 'nuclear reactor'
- Use the advanced section of your search engine
- Use the + sign between keywords to link them, for example typing + KS3 after your keyword will help you find web pages at the right level.

Where to search

Search engine

A search engine looks through the entire web and lists all sites that match the words in the search box. It can give thousands of links, but the best matches are at the top of the list, on the first page. Try **bbc.co.uk/search**

Search directory

A search directory is like a library of websites that have been sorted by a person instead of a computer. You can search by keyword or subject and browse through the different sites like you look through books on a library shelf. A good example is **yahooligans.com**

45

Glossary

AGR advanced gas-cooled reactor

alpha radiation radiation made from two protons and two neutrons stuck together

atom tiny particle that everything is made from

background radiation radiation that is all around us

ban not allow something to happen

beta radiation radiation made from fast-moving electrons from the nucleus

billion one thousand million

cancer disease caused by cells growing out of control

cargo ship ship that carries goods around the world

cell tiny object that living things are made from

chain reaction nuclear reaction that keeps itself going

chemical reaction reaction where the same elements join together in different ways

compound substance made from two or more elements chemically joined together

contaminated spoiled

control rod part of a nuclear reactor that control the speed of the reaction

coolant gas or liquid that takes the heat away from the reactor core

critical mass amount of radioactive metal needed for a steady nuclear reaction

curium very radioactive, rare metal

decommissioned taken out of service and closed down

DNA chemical that carries information that cells need to work properly

Earth's core centre part of the Earth

efficient able to do a job without wasting a lot of energy

electron tiny negatively-charged particle found in atoms

element substance made from only one type of atom

energy ability to do work. Light, heat and electricity are types of energy.

expand get bigger

fallout substances that are made in an explosion and fall to the ground

fatal something that kills you

fossil fuel coal, oil or natural gas

fuel cell device that makes electricity from chemical reactions

fuel substance that stores energy and releases it when burned

gamma radiation radiation made using powerful invisible energy

gamma scan medical scan made with gamma radiation

generator equipment used to make electricity

genetic to do with information in cells

geothermal anything to do with heat from deep underground

global warming extra warming of the Earth caused by an increased greenhouse effect

graphite type of carbon found in pencils

gravity force that pulls everything together and keeps us on the ground

greenhouse effect keeping the atmosphere warm by trapping heat

greenhouse gas gas that is good at trapping heat

half-life time it takes for half the atoms in a sample of radioactive material to break up

icebreaker ship that clears ice from the surface of the sea

infra-red invisible heat energy

irradiated exposed to radiation

kinetic energy energy of all moving things

Latin ancient language used by the Romans

lunar to do with the moon

meltdown when nuclear fuel gets so hot that it melts

mineral substance needed by plants and animals in small amounts to keep them healthy

mutations changes to DNA and cells

neutron sub-atomic particle found in the nucleus of an atom

nuclear anything to do with the nucleus of an atom

nuclear fission splitting atoms

nuclear fusion nuclear reaction where the nuclei of two atoms join together

nuclear reaction reaction involving the nucleus of an atom

nuclear reactor structure for making heat using radioactive substances

nuclei word for more than one nucleus

nucleus centre of an atom

particle tiny bit

particle accelerator machine that accelerates sub-atomic particles to very high speeds

polar ice caps ice covering the North and South Poles of the Earth

predict make an informed guess that something will happen

protest go on marches or demonstrations to show that you do not agree with something

proton sub-atomic particle found in the nucleus of an atom

PWR pressurized water reactor

radiation type of energy in the form of rays, waves or particles

radioactive something that can give off radiation

ray beam of light or radiation

reactor core main part of a nuclear reactor

reactor vessel container for the reactor core

reprocessing making new nuclear fuel from used nuclear fuel

rover moving machine for collecting information about a planet or moon

RTG short for radioisotope thermoelectric generator, a type of nuclear battery

shipping lane route taken by ships from one port to another

spring running water from the ground

sterilized object without any living bacteria on or in it

sub-atomic particles tiny bits that make atoms

surgical instrument equipment used by surgeons

tracer substance that is easy to track inside the body

tumour lump caused by cancer cells

turbine machinery that is turned by moving air, water or steam

unstable likely to break up

vacuum empty space with nothing in it, not even air

waste unwanted material left behind

weapon tests testing weapons to check that they work properly

Index

Series in the *Freestyle Curriculum Strand* include:

Turbulent Planet

Energy Essentials

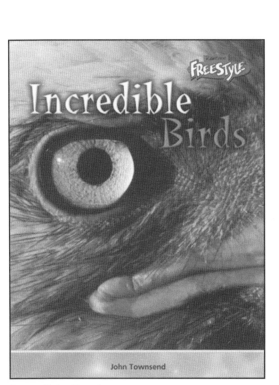

Incredible Creatures

Material Matters

Find out about the other titles in these series on our website www.raintreepublishers.co.uk